Life is Strange and so are You

Life is Strange and so are You

**Andrews McMeel
Publishing**

Kansas City

by Dan Piraro

01 02 03 04 05 QUD 10 9 8 7 6 5 4 3 2 1

ISBN: 0-7407-1848-7

Library of Congress Catalog Card Number: 2001087672

ATTENTION: SCHOOLS AND BUSINESSES

Andrews McMeel books are available at quantity discounts with bulk purchase for educational, business, or sales promotional use. For information, please write to: Special Sales Department, Andrews McMeel Publishing, 4520 Main Street, Kansas City, Missouri 64111.

This book is dedicated to that guy in the car next to me at the light yesterday.
He looked like he could use it.

Special thanks to my parents for screwing me up just enough to be a cartoonist.

Thanks to Katherine Baronet for all her design help.

Table of Contents

Introduction

As I sit in the dark, dank, cavernous lower level of the vast underground cartoon archives beneath my fourteen-room luxury mobile home in downtown Dallas, it occurs to me that in the fifteen years I have been drawing *Bizarro* I have accumulated far more Sunday cartoons than I could possibly cram into one book, unless, of course, that book were as thick as this sentence is long.

So instead I've chosen a few of my favorites, most of them from the past couple of years. The more recent ones are better, to my mind—funnier, tighter, and artistically better resolved—and many of the older ones have been nibbled to bits by rats.

In compiling them I considered a number of options but decided in the end to arrange them more or less chronologically. I think it is infinitely more interesting to see how a person's work has evolved over the years than, for instance, to see two cartoons about teenagers on facing pages, then a couple of jokes about dog poo on the next two pages, etc.

At the bottom of most pages there are notes I've written about each cartoon. These notes make a little more sense if read in the order they appear throughout the book. Included in this book is the genesis of each of the recurring symbols so many people wonder about today, and the notes at the bottom identify when and why those symbols began. At the back of this book are a couple of pages dedicated to explaining the symbols in detail and some fun and useful activities associated with them.

Contrary to the beliefs of many of my readers, I am not at all wealthy. Accordingly, I hope you enjoy this book, hope you buy a hundred copies, and hope you persuade a hundred of your closest friends to do the same. Maybe then I can quit my day job as a bologna distributor.

Your pal,
Dan Piraro

This cartoon was the first of several *Family Circus* spoofs I've done. I hadn't met Bil Keane at this time and nearly swallowed my tongue when he called me the next day. Fortunately, he's a great guy, loves *Family Circus* satires, and was calling to see if I would give him the original. I traded it to him for one of his Sunday drawings.

I like this joke, and was thrilled with the way the coloring turned out. Back then, I was using the traditional system of coloring whereby the artist provides a black-and-white image with dozens (or hundreds) of color-by-number call outs to be interpreted by someone else, from which film is then produced and given to the client papers to print. I never knew how the color would really look until it came out in the paper weeks later.

I am a fan of anthropology and primitive culture and had to draw upon my limited knowledge in this area to defend this cartoon against accusations of racism and racial stereotyping from a handful of readers around the country. Anticipating such a response, I intentionally put a clean-cut, African American couple at the table at left for contrast. The tribesmen in the background are meant to represent those from New Guinea, many of whom still look this way. I find them fascinating and incredibly cool looking and was pleased to find a way to get them into a cartoon.

I've always enjoyed including other cartoon characters in my work, and this one about the very common "desert island" cartoon motif was a lot of fun to create. Each of the characters are taken from real cartoonists. Some are easier to identify than others; see page 140 for the answers.

I still love this joke after all these years. On the same day, a week after it ran, I received two letters—one criticizing me for being insensitive to the plight of amputees, the other from a prosthetics company who wanted to put the image on t-shirts to use as promotional items. They mentioned that many of their customers thought it was hilarious.

A fun gag with a fun picture, especially the super-sexy ad on the back of the bus featuring me when I looked like a freak. This was when I was inviting readers to e-mail me, which eventually led to my infamous all-mooch book tour financed by my fans. I solicited free plane tickets, meals, rides, and places to stay from the folks who had e-mailed me over the previous couple of years. I wrote about the experience in a book called *Bizarro Among the Savages*.

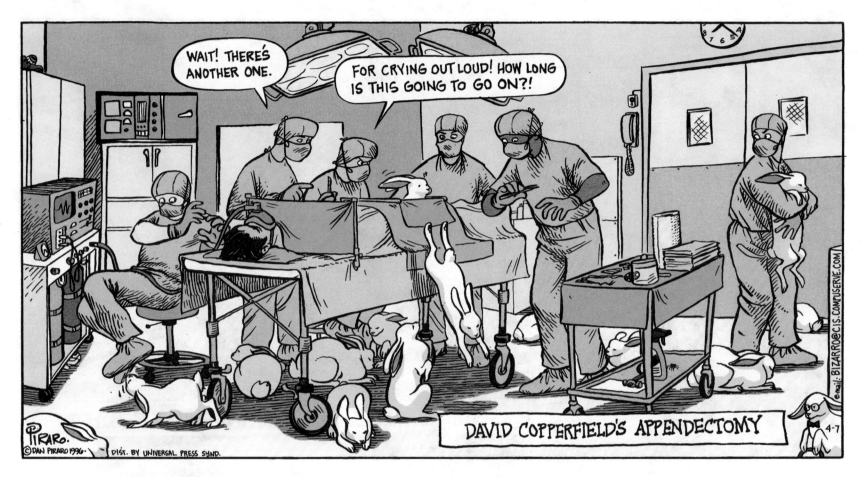

This drawing was one of the very first where I began to hide things in the picture that don't relate to the punch line directly. David Copperfield himself bought the original to this cartoon. I always think it's cool when that happens. Here are a few others who have my work: Sheryl Crow, Dick Clark, Penn and Teller, Sherwood Schwartz, Pixar Studios. How many out-of-place objects can you find in this picture? Answer is on page 140.

I'm a fan of trompe l'oeil and regularly use it in my fine art.
The character doing the painting is a caricature of me back in '96,
when I had long hair and a ridiculous Salvador Dalí mustache.

©DAN PIRARO ·1996· DIST. BY UNIVERSAL PRESS SYND. PIRARO 7-7

I loathe repetition of almost any kind, so it is fun for me to step outside of my style from time to time. The line work, character design, and coloring in this one were fun steps away from the more realistic drawings I was usually doing at the time.

I had fun with the art and alternative coloring on this one. It is also one of those rare jokes I've written that has less than 250 words.

Most readers were able to solve this puzzle quickly. If you have trouble finding Waldo, however, the answer is on page 140.

After sixteen years of marriage I went through an unscheduled, surprise divorce in 1996. The subject crept up in my daily cartoons during the process and I found it to be a great way to blow off steam. My ex-wife was angry that I was portraying our personal life in the paper, which, of course, only made it more fun to do.

I think my cartoons are often too complex for the average American armchair zombie and this is a perfect example. I still really like this idea, but I'm guessing I lost more than a few comics readers somewhere around the forty-third paragraph.

This cartoon represents the sort of existence I most fear. For me, eternity like this would not be "Heck," but full-blown, tear-your-eyeballs-out Hell.

Here I was beginning to experiment with more creative solutions to coloring. Under the old system of providing only a black-and-white image with color-by-number call outs for the printer to follow, none of the images outside the window actually appeared on the original drawing. They were sketched in pencil, assigned colors, and explained in writing to the print technician. I had to wait for the cartoon to appear in the paper to see if it worked the way I had envisioned. I was pretty happy with the results. The character in the back saying, "Air!..." is me shortly after I cut my hair and shaved the Dalí mustache.

I like this kind of cartoon that requires you to look carefully to get the gag. The two characters walking behind the yellow street pole at left are me and my then-girlfriend, Kristine. "Miss Freckles" was her cat. Not long after my divorce I found that putting a woman (or her cat) in your cartoon is a far more effective aphrodisiac than any sports car.

A good gag wherein the picture appears to be telling a completely different story than what is actually happening.
The characters at right are me and my then-girlfriend, Kristine. The names on the name tags represent friends of hers.

I sat down one day and figured out how to create a simple "magic eye" illusion and drew this entirely by hand. It works best if you hold it about eighteen inches away and cross your eyes, instead of looking "through" it, which is usually the way to get better results. It doesn't make a new picture like the real Magic Eye, but it does create a pretty good artificial sense of depth. The characters are from my sketch book and personally I don't think the joke itself is all that funny. I did this panel mostly just for the challenge of creating 3-D by hand.

The character at far right is me, though I'm not sure why I colored myself so dark. Might have been a mistake, I don't remember. The lady in front of me in line is a woman I was serving jury duty with when I drew this.

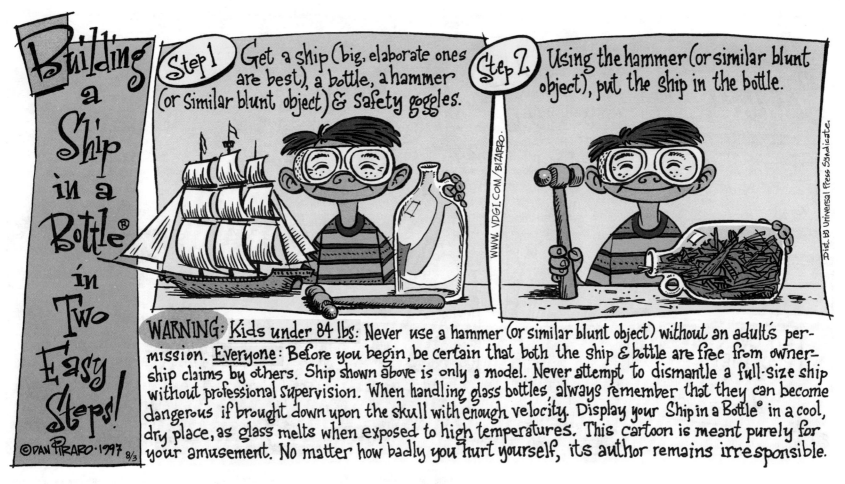

Building a Ship in a Bottle® in Two Easy Steps!

©DAN PIRARO·1997 8/3

Step 1 Get a ship (big, elaborate ones are best), a bottle, a hammer (or similar blunt object) & safety goggles.

Step 2 Using the hammer (or similar blunt object), put the ship in the bottle.

WWW.VDGI.COM/BIZARRO

Dist. by Universal Press Syndicate

WARNING: Kids under 84 lbs: Never use a hammer (or similar blunt object) without an adult's permission. Everyone: Before you begin, be certain that both the ship & bottle are free from ownership claims by others. Ship shown above is only a model. Never attempt to dismantle a full-size ship without professional supervision. When handling glass bottles, always remember that they can become dangerous if brought down upon the skull with enough velocity. Display your Ship in a Bottle® in a cool, dry place, as glass melts when exposed to high temperatures. This cartoon is meant purely for your amusement. No matter how badly you hurt yourself, its author remains irresponsible.

This gag is hideously long-winded, as much of my work is. Still, I love writing humorous instructions for things. On airplanes I frequently draw cartoon instructions on the airsick bags and return them to their pocket. This cartoon was among the first "instructional," "game," or "activity" related cartoons that I have done. I enjoy that genre a lot, my favorite being the "find three things wrong with this picture" cartoons (see pages 38, 88, and 102).

A fun satire of the golden age of altruistic, talking animal shows which I used to watch when I was growing up. Even as a kid, I wondered how anyone could tell the difference between Lassie's Timmy-is-trapped-under-a-bus bark, and her I-heard-a-mailbox-lid-slam-four-blocks-away bark.

Here I began to experiment with ways to get a sense of depth by using colored lines in the background instead of black. I still love the idea behind this joke.

33

This is a weird idea that is totally lost if the reader cannot recite that old "this old man, he played one" song. But I've never shied away from obscure ideas, which my real die-hard fans love but which is also a big part of why I'm not rich. The blue sketch in the corner of the page is from my original idea page that I use when writing jokes.

I love the look of this cartoon, especially the goofy old Thunderbird, one my favorite cars ever. For my money, you can keep the tasteful '50s T-birds and give me a "space-age" land yacht from the '60s any old day.

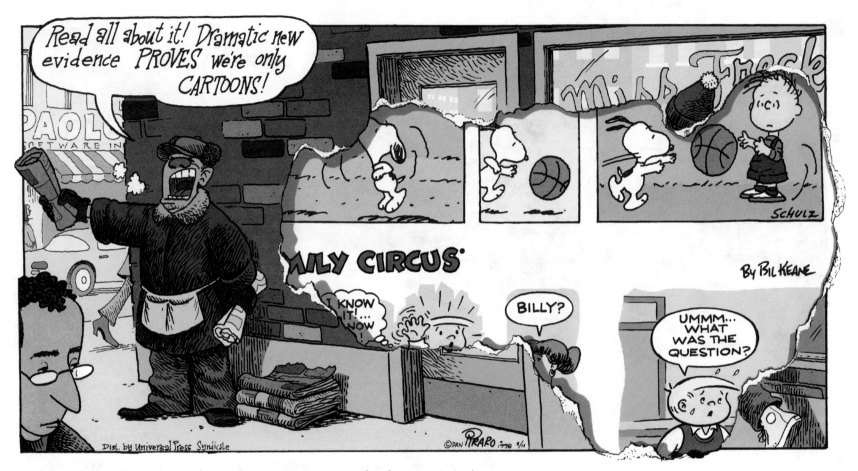

A little fun with trompe l'oeil and using other people's comics in my own, two of my favorite pastimes. The comics on the next page were drawn by hand, incidentally, not photocopied and pasted in. That's me in the lower left corner. I put myself in a lot of comics fully realizing that no one knows it is me unless they've met me. I do it partly as a nod to Alfred Hitchcock and partly because I look like a cartoon character and don't have to exaggerate much to fit myself in.

I particularly like the art on this one. The green line work inside the light beam works really well, I think. This was created in the traditional method of designating colors by number, then hoping it looks right when it comes out in the paper, so that made it a particularly satisfying success. Though I've never worked in a corporate environment and don't personally relate to most *Dilbert* cartoons, I think Scott Adams is a real genius.

Can You Find 3 Things Wr[ong?]

Miss Freckles' School for the Exceptionally Precious

...believes professional wrestling is real. ③ Cat has been awake for more than 15 minutes in a row.

This was the first of several I've done in this motif, and represents my favorite kind of Sunday comic. Lots to look at, plenty of weirdness, a puzzle motif, and what I consider to be some pretty good punch lines. It also gives me a chance to inject some social editorial content. The fishlike characters in the upper right corner are me and my then-girlfriend, Kristine.

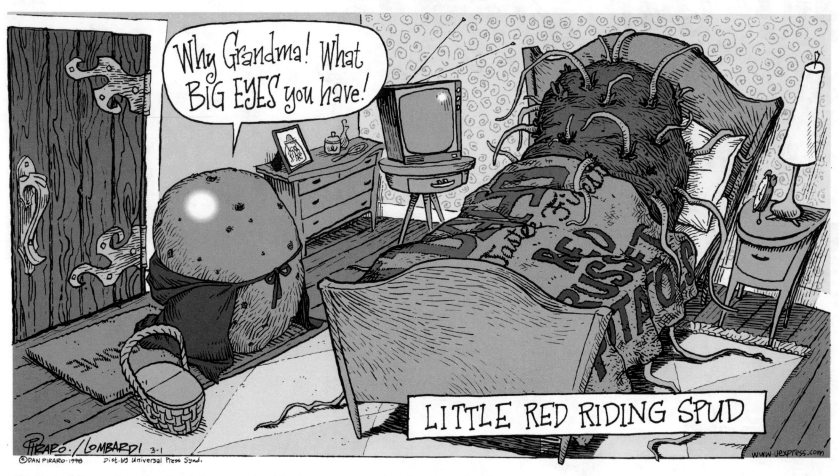

This is one of the rare times when I've used someone else's idea for a cartoon. I get lots of suggestions for jokes, several each week, but normally only use one or two each year. This one was written by my then-girlfriend, Kristine.

This was my first really successful attempt at using color to suggest depth. It isn't perfect, but the background here recedes into the distance quite well. I also like the joke, which pokes fun at the gun-control issue. I'm often tempted to come out more forcefully against the NRA in my comics, but I'm afraid someone will shoot me.

Once again, my arm is EXHAUSTED & they STILL won't give us their valuables!

IF GUNS ARE INVENTED, ONLY INVENTORS WILL HAVE GUNS

ANTHONY DODGES THE LAW WHILE KEN DUCKS THE COPS

I really like this picture, the play of light and dark, and the weird puns.
Puns only work for me when they are very strange and unexpected.

Another game motif, which I do as often as I can think of one. This one is fairly subtle, especially the line "all the locals have an accent," and I imagine many readers missed it entirely. My favorite part is the drawing of the tourist family in the upper left. This cartoon was written while on a trip to London with my two daughters, Krullspeth and Klimert.

Here is another example of referring to other cartoons, and a pretty successful joke I think. Not so successful is the attempt to suggest different depths with color. The guy in the right foreground (who is reading one of my books) should have had black line work instead of purple. Even worse is that for some ludicrous reason it never occurred to me until I saw it in the paper that the blue sleeping guy in the background looks as though his head is coming out of the flight attendant's butt.

You Can Draw a Clown!

Tools: ① Drawing surface (paper, wall, bald head, etc.) ② Drawing thing (chalk, crayon, pencil, charred stick) ③ Sense of humor (optional) READY? LET'S DRAW!

STEP A. Draw a circle on top of a lump.

STEP 2. Add funny stuff you've seen on clowns.

Goofy hair.

Nose glasses.

Backward hat.

←Oversized shirt & huge, baggy pants are a MUST.

Big, clunky shoes

©DAN PIRARO·1998

STEP III. Add whatever is missing... (arms, chin, spleen, etc.)

...and you've drawn a clown!

WHoops! I seem to have drawn film critic Gene Shalit dressed like an average American teenager by mistake. Oh well... Sometimes the best art is accidental!

4-26

Dist. by Universal Press Synd.   www.uexpress.com

Here is another game activity spoof, which grew out of Lord-knows-what thought process. I still think it is funny. The little blue guy at lower left is me.

45

This idea sprang from the fact that I speak at a lot of public schools, often on career day. I love talking to school kids, except middle school–age kids, who should all be shipped out to sea until they are in high school.

This has long been one of my favorite gags and drawings. My favorite parts are the diagrams in the background, which could barely be read in the paper. They say: "The Brain and Its Accessories," "Locating and Identifying the Brain" (the label pointing to the head says "Brain," the rest all say "No"), and "Your Eyeball, Your Friend."

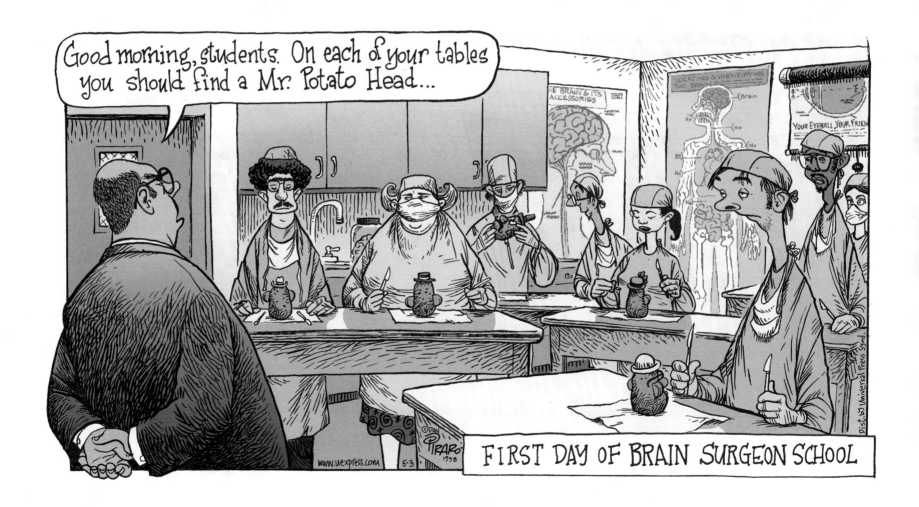

47

Magic Nose
3-D Smellusion®

1. Hold the MAGIC NOSE 3-D SMELLUSION® at arm's length.
2. Slowly move it closer to your face until your nose touches the red "X."
3. Close your eyes & inhale deeply...

What do you smell?
(answer below)

X

© DAN PIRARO · 1998 ⁴⁷ Dist. by Universal Press Synd.   WWW. UEXPRESS.COM   MAGIC NOSE 3-D SMELLUSION® ANSWER: carpool

AUTHOR'S NOTE: The dog-like creature in this episode is NOT international pop-culture sensation, SQUEEKY the TALKING CHIHUAHUA, but his half-wit cousin, TROY the YAPPING BONEHEAD.

For a while I was using this strange typeface every time an extraterrestrial spoke. I gave it up eventually because it was a pain in the neck to write and hard to read in longer captions. I also put a "mediocrity rules" T-shirt in a number of comics around this time. This was my first recurring background joke. Don't miss the author's note at the bottom of the cartoon. Can you name three other vegetables that aliens frequently come to earth as? Answer on page 140.

This one combines two of my favorite activities, game spoofs and social commentary. I like the drawings a lot, especially B, F, and G, but the coloring came out a little garish. The blue and orange worms around the title are not at all what I tried to convey in my instructions to the printer technician, but that is the risk you take with the traditional coloring method. In mid-2000 I switched to coloring them myself on computer to alleviate this sort of Sunday morning surprise.

One of a number of *Family Circus* spoofs I've done. The original drawing of this one belongs to the real "Jeffy," now a six-foot-something hunk of a guy you'd never guess was the cute little round-headed kid in the comics. He introduced himself to me at a cartoonists' convention one year and we've been friends ever since. Maybe the high point of my career as a cartoonist was when my name was featured in a *Family Circus* cartoon. Billy says, "The Piraro's dad wears gold chains and an earring. All our dad wears is glasses and deodorant." F.Y.I. I wear earrings, but I've never worn a gold chain.

REDNECKS TAMPERING WITH PHYSICS

That's me behind the wheel of the orange car. Having grown up in Oklahoma I was all too often the victim of rednecks with supernatural powers. Can you guess how many times I was beaten up by hillbillies when I was growing up? Answer is on page 140.

In the lower left section of this cartoon you'll see a note about Squeeky the Original Talking Chihuahua. I've never had recurring characters in my cartoons, thus making my work harder to license and market in other areas, and had often used Squeeky as a sort of recurring satire pointing out that fact. I had been doing this for several years before the Taco Bell talking Chihuahua was created and often pointed it out in the comics, lest anyone think I was stealing from them. An interesting side note: Taco Bell's advertising was handled by a company based in Dallas, where I lived at this time. For the year or so prior to the advent of their talking dog campaign, I was dating a woman who worked at that very agency and socialized with dozens of people who worked there. Coincidence?

SUNDAY COMICS CROSS WORDS PUZZLE!!

WWW.UEXPRESS.COM
Distributed by Universal Press Syndicate

DOWN

1. Dad yells this in traffic.
2. Especially useful after stubbing your toe.
3. What Mom calls Dad when he phones from Happy Hour.
4. Colorful reference to the dog that barks all night.
5. Grandpa's name for the guy who got his old job. (obs.)
7. Gets bleeped from every episode of the Jerry Springer show.

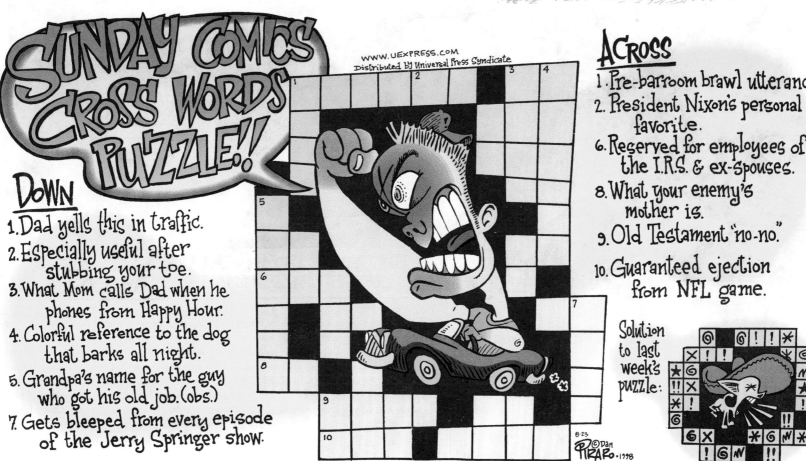

ACROSS

1. Pre-barroom brawl utterance.
2. President Nixon's personal favorite.
6. Reserved for employees of the I.R.S. & ex-spouses.
8. What your enemy's mother is.
9. Old Testament "no-no."
10. Guaranteed ejection from NFL game.

Solution to last week's puzzle:

8-23
© DAN PIRARO · 1998

54

I like the drawings of the characters in this, some of whom were taken from life. The "pessimist" is how I look when I've gotten a bad haircut; the "alarmist" is my fourth grade teacher; the "pugilist" is based on my tenth grade gym coach; the "antagonist" is one of those rednecks with supernatural powers I referred to on page 52.

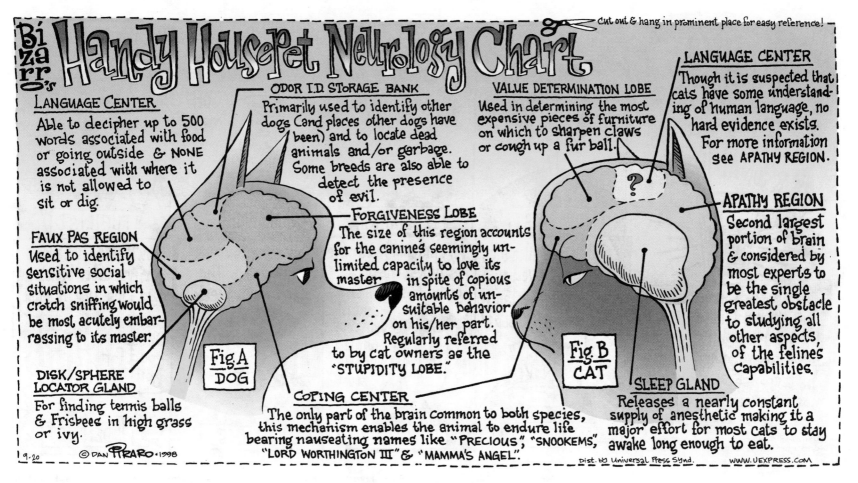

Another prime example of my unquenchable verbosity, but a very popular cartoon with my readers, nonetheless.

I have a friend in Tulsa, Oklahoma, named Virginia, who is the self-proclaimed president and founder of the Dan Piraro Fan Club. She's around seventy years old or so and travels all over the world doing the most incredible things. Her living room is full of small bits of things she has stolen from all over the world, a stone from the Great Wall of China, one from the Pyramids in Egypt, etc. This cartoon is a tribute to her amusing difficulty with honoring the unwritten boundaries between herself and world-renowned monuments.

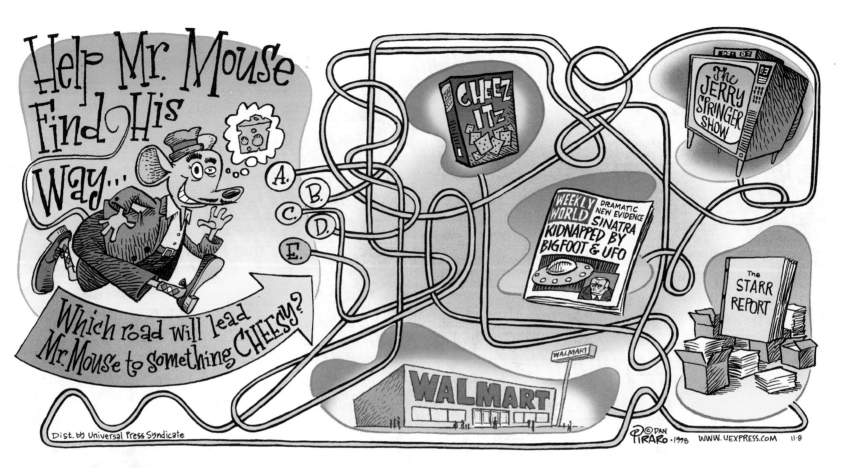

The only correct answer to this puzzle is, of course, "all of the above."

An adult survivor of Catholic school, I enjoy doing takeoffs on religion and bible stories. Most people relate well to these and enjoy them; a few take exception and command me to stop making fun of God. I always wonder how these readers came to the belief that humor was created by the devil. Don't miss the print on Moses' swimsuit.

Godzilla vs. Barney the Dinosaur
THIS TIME TERROR IS BACK IN A RUBBER SUIT!

This drawing reflects that part of me that has never grown up and still enjoys depicting demolished cars and stuff. Like any fully functional human over the age of seven, I detest Barney the Dinosaur.

I had a great time with the composition of this strip and still enjoy the story line. Since it is about letters, here's a real challenge: How many times does the letter "e" appear in this book? Answer is on page 140.

Any time I need a couple extra bucks, I do a cartoon about doctors or lawyers—someone almost always buys the original. For some reason, doctors and especially lawyers love jokes about themselves. Maybe it's an ego thing. Hmmm . . .

Pixar Studios in California bought the original drawing of this for their office.

This one is a strange idea that I happened across while brainstorming for jokes one day. Since the earth is a sphere, wouldn't a "bottomless pit" have to come out on the other side? And given the way gravity works, wouldn't you just keep falling back and forth? I'm sure most people got it, but I had to explain this one to a number of readers who wrote in.

This is my favorite spoof of another cartoon I've ever done.
It was particularly fun because I'm not a very big fan of Garfield.

A few months before this cartoon was drawn I started dating Katherine, who is, at this writing, still my girlfriend. That's her standing in the front row looking onto the stage. This is the first drawing of her of many that have appeared in my cartoons. Sitting next to where she got up from is me.

I have participated in a number of charity auctions wherein people bid for the opportunity to be in a future *Bizarro* cartoon. This was one such cartoon, purchased for Colin by his parents as a birthday or Christmas present. Colin is a very bright kid and an excellent magician, so this cartoon particularly fit his personality.

The woman in this cartoon is Katherine again, this is (basically) her apartment, and the critter speaking the punch line is her cat, Trixie. The small brown and orange dog on the sofa is Steve, my Papillon, and the skinny gray and white one on the blue chair is my Italian Greyhound, Bruno.

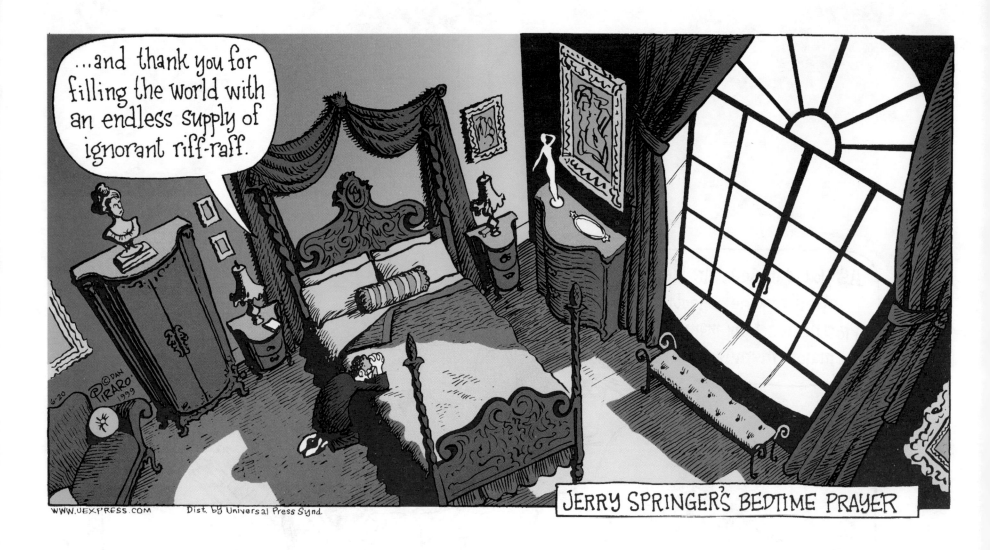

This cartoon marks the beginning of the recurring symbols. The crown and "ExC" (both of which referred to my girlfriend, Katherine) appear on the windows at left, a "k" is on the orange awning (which later became "k2") and is a reference to my daughters, whose names are Klondyke and Krapuzar. "ExC" is an abbreviation of a nickname I have for Katherine, which is too saccharin to print. Mr. P's Rent-a-Sherpa is an inside joke with Katherine because she is constantly finding extremely heavy things for me to carry for her.

Students of art history get this one, most other people don't. Another reason why I'm not a millionaire.

This was one of my daily comics back in the '80s, which I redrew for a Sunday comic in '99 because I liked it. The pictures on the wall at left are characters drawn by an underground cartoonist called "Kaz." His name also appears in a headline in the paper the man is reading. I've never met him, but I like his work and was reading some of it at the time I drew this cartoon. This drawing marks the beginning of my habit of routinely putting as many strange elements in backgrounds as I can.

I love this joke because you have to think about it. Some people get it immediately, some after some thought, many never get it at all and have to ask. If you can't figure it out, see page 140 for the answer. Keep in mind that it might be simpler than you think.

FRANKENSTEIN VISITS CALIFORNIA

This is one of the best examples of my passion for packing lots of funny lines in background billboards, ads, magazine covers, and newspaper headlines. My favorite one is the investment ad.

Bobby, Hector, Hilary, and Weldon are all friends of mine. We get together occasionally for a "boys night" and Hector almost routinely cancels at the last minute for one reason or another. Hence, he became the little piggy who stayed home.

I am well known among my friends and family for despising the tacky, commercialized mess that is modern-day American Christmas, hence this cartoon. A couple of personal notes: The woman driving the blue car at the extreme left is my girlfriend and there is a muffin on top of her car because at that time I was in the habit of bringing her a muffin at work every day. The groovy Vespa scooter at right is mine, which I have had since it was new in 1980 and still ride whenever the weather permits. Notice the appearance of the bird with the hat (but not yet upside down) in the lower right by the signature. This is likely the first drawing of him.

A kid at a local high school that I spoke at recently told me that this was the funniest cartoon he'd ever seen, so I put it in the book. Notice the bird on the mantle, not yet upside down.

Lots of hidden jokes in the background here and the first official appearance of many of the recurring symbols all together. The crown is in her skirt, the bird is on the lower shelf of the table, not yet being drawn upside down, but there is one in the tree that is (the first). The eyeball is behind the firemen, and there are two aliens in the bushes, but without spaceships.

There are a number of hidden jokes in this panel, along with my scooter, the bird,
the crown, a fish, and the eyeball. Don't miss the brain coming out of the football player on TV.

The half-witted earthling on the alien's video screen is me. The multi-legged aliens were fashioned after my former mother-in-law (drawn from memory).

One of my favorite cartoons I've done, and definitely my favorite game motif. Lots to look at here, plenty of fun characters, and TWO Vespas! The only thing I regret is that the printer guys misunderstood my coloring directions and made the sky red violet instead of blue violet. It really messes up the color composition, but what can you do? Also, less noticeable, the sky beneath the flying saucer should be yellow, like the surrounding sky, not lime green like the saucer glass. Bummer. The big character on the left in the red suit is featured prominently on the home page of my new Web site.

ings Wrong with this Picture?

ANSWERS: ①There is not a single STARBUCKS in sight. ②Happy

THE PANTOMIME NEWS NETWORK

Someone once said that the lottery is a tax on people who are bad at math. I couldn't agree more and drew this cartoon based on that notion. Ms. Lafferty is a local school teacher who has been having me come speak to her class every year for nearly a decade now (notice the yellow poster on the wall at right) and I gave the original drawing of this to her. The background is full of lots of fun stuff, and the recurring symbols are firmly in place.

This is the first cartoon I ever colored on computer myself, instead of using the traditional method. In this way I can control the colors better and see what it is going to look like before I send it in. This first time took me forever but it represents a huge step forward in my ability to get the kind of art I want in my Sunday comics. My favorite element of this cartoon is the chimp in briefs. This may also be the first time I drew the "bunny head" in the background.

Another highway sign cartoon, also with my scooter. If you don't currently have a Vespa, you should get one.

The title box at left ran with all my cartoons (in cities where they use this size title box) from about 1990 till 2000. After I learned to color my own Sundays, I began designing new title boxes almost every week. The first one (at right) was an update of the original, and is used as a sort of default box on weeks when I don't create a new one.

Any time you can combine biblical themes with public nudity in the Sunday paper and get away with it, you've done a full day's work.

With my passion for charts and diagrams, it wasn't long before I used that theme in a title box, along with the main elements of my recurring symbols. These boxes only print in a very small handful of cities, so most people never get to see them. I do them mostly to entertain myself.

I like this gag a lot and hoped people would enjoy finding the differences between the two frames.
I particularly like the rubber glove box labels, which say, "unpleasant task gloves" and "rubber chicken hats."

Probably the most elaborate title box I've ever done, this took
me more time to ink and color than the panel it ran with.

Over a period of three weeks or so in the summer of 2000, I wrote several dozen odd children's poems in a sketch book of mine. I intend to publish them as a book at some point, but in the meantime I used a few for Sunday cartoons. This was the first one of that series that I used.

My favorite books are by Dr. Seuss—
I remember the one about the
skateboarding moose,

or was
it a goose
in a yellow
caboose?

PATOOT!

or maybe a GROBNITZ
who coughs up PATOOTS?

Dist. by Universal Press Synd.

And who could forget the
SCHMOODLE-PUNK BUNYONS,

who ate
only CAR
PARTS prepared with
grilled onions.

I remember
the CAT WHO WAS
FAT who came back...
...or emailed, or called up,
or something like that.

uexpress.com   ©DAN PIRARO. 2000. 7-9

But my favorite Seuss
was a story he drew

about a hippo named
HORTON who sang
for THE WHO.

Another of the children's poems I wrote and later used as a Sunday cartoon. This one was very popular with readers, primarily, I think, because Seuss is so popular. I, myself, am a huge fan of Seuss's writing and drawing.

From time to time I use the name of someone I know and/or admire in my cartoons. When I wrote this joke, it seemed vaguely like something a character in *Ballard Street* would do, so I used Jerry Van Amerongen's name in it. He appreciated it and traded me one of his original drawings for this one. There are some fun headlines on the stuff on the table, and a magazine title I use frequently, "Spoiled Athletes Weekly."

This is the third "find three things wrong" cartoon and much of this illustration was later used on my Web site. You'll recognize the guy on the TV from the cover of this book, as well as the little scooter guy.

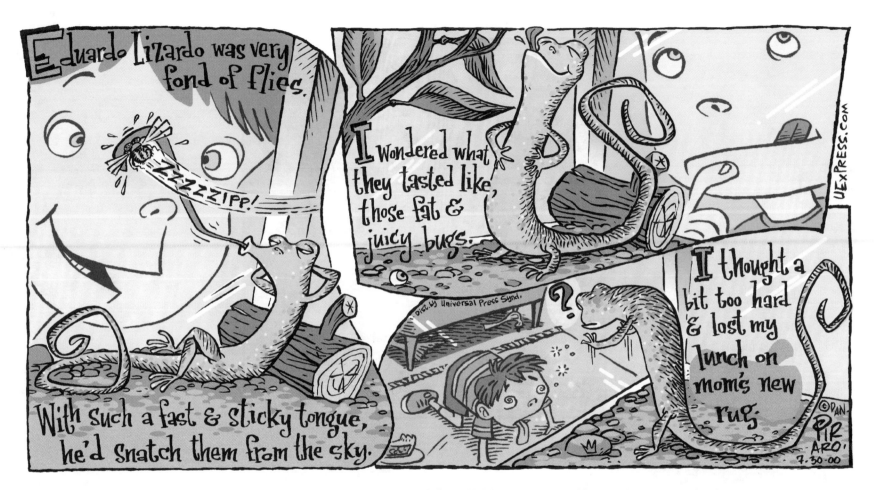

The third of the odd children's poems I used for a Sunday comic. My daughters used to have a lizard just like this named Eduardo Lizardo. I used to stalk piles of dog poop in the yard with a butterfly net every day to catch flies for him. I actually enjoyed it, it became a sort of sport, but my neighbors thought I was a psycho.

Here I am able to combine two of my great loves; monkeys and scooters. Monkeys figure fairly prominently as a contrasting metaphor for humans in many of my cartoons and much of my personal fine art.

I loved this box and the cartoon that went with it but my local paper bumped *Bizarro* on the day it was supposed to run for one of those lovely color ads for above-ground swimming pools. I never got to see it in print until this book. This same image was used for the cover of a Norwegian *Bizarro* book.

I still love the look of this drawing, especially the big-headed idiot on the left. I've always thought it would be fun to get on *Who Wants to Be a Millionaire* or *Win Ben Stein's Money* but haven't been able to. Sadly, I'm not nearly enough of a celebrity to get on the celebrity version of those shows.

My style of traditional joke writing doesn't lend itself well to outrageous character drawings so it is particularly fun for me to be able to cut loose on some of these puzzle-type gags. Incidentally, there is still time to enter this contest; to my knowledge no winner has been named since it came out. See page 140 for details.

This panel has some of my favorite background jokes. The signs are fun, especially the one about pig noises. I like the guy obsessed with licorice, and the pie Polaroid in the hand of yours truly in the foreground. Notice also that each character is colored monochromatically, except the dog. (For the reason, see page 140.) Also worth noting is that "licorice" in this sentence is spelled differently than in the cartoon. See page 140 for this reason too.

This is my shot at the phenomenal marketing success of shallowness and stupidity in America. If people will pay over five dollars for a Beanie Baby, why can't I get rich off Scamp!?

Here is another of the children's poems I wrote. It is one of the most obscure ones I've written and I still wonder if many people could follow it. All of the names, facts, and caricatures in this cartoon are completely true to life.

Not a particularly engaging drawing on this one but a cool idea. I've always fantasized about saving someone's life with the Heimlich maneuver and being a big hero. I saw a man perform this on a woman at a party once and it worked perfectly. She was able to clear her windpipe of the offending cocktail onion and regain her breath, then she promptly vomited on the floor. She left in shame moments later and the guy who saved her left shortly thereafter. Nothing puts a damper on a party like a puddle of regurgitated tortilla chips from the snack table.

As is often the case, the background jokes are my favorite in this one. I love creating phony headlines and book titles. *Bizarro Among the Cabbages* is a spoof of my own book, *Bizarro Among the Savages*. I still get a giggle out of *Where's Mildew?*

To my surprise, this cartoon turned out to be a lot of people's favorite for some reason. Apparently lots of folks have a soft spot for angry bunnies.

I got the idea for this titlebox from my day job as a bologna distributor. I used to import it also, but I got out of it a few years ago because it was just too much of a hassle. My dream is to one day have my own brand, like the one in the picture.

More fun with medical charts, a couple with really bad puns. I have an open mind about acupuncture but can't resist having some fun with the various fringe element beliefs about medical treatment. In some corner of America (probably in California) someone no doubt believes in the healing powers of foot stomping.

WAY DOWN YONDER ON THE GENETICALLY ALTERED CROP FARM

This gag proved very popular with readers. I enjoy this kind of drawing because it gives me lots of room to create weird characters and hide background jokes. That's me with the arrow through my head.

This is one of my favorite title boxes ever, and I used these characters
very prominently on the home page of my Web site at BIZARRO.COM.

Maybe I'm wrong, but I think an idea like this taxes the average *Garfield* fan beyond their capabilities. I personally love a joke that takes some imagination to complete. As a member of the fine arts community (outside of cartooning) I also love taking shots at pretentious performance artists.

I experimented with color on this one and like the end result for the most part. However, if I had colored the wall and swinging door of the saloon in a blue or violet hue instead of the pale green, it would have really driven home the dark-inside/light-outside effect I was going for. Dang.

To my mind, there is almost no geekier job than TV weatherman. I've used them in cartoons quite a lot over the years, but I particularly like this connection between a meteorologist and being hit by a meteor. I also like the "another trendy shallow night spot" sign in the background. That's me and Katherine to the right of center: me in my Vespa jacket, her with red hair.

135

The colors on this are intentionally offset, a style which I personally like a lot.
But it always worries me that some readers might think it was an accident.

I was particularly happy with the way this one came out, especially the green lighting. For the second time, all my symbols except one are in formaldehyde. This is one of those rare cartoon ideas that was taken from life; I've had to go through this same process with my own skateboarding daughters, Krugeragn and Kholstoof, more times than I care to count.

I'm a real fan of contemporary and retro-contemporary furniture from the '50s and '60s. The couch in this drawing was one I had on order but had not yet arrived, except mine is gray. The lamps are fantasies, which I'm still looking for. The two end tables are from my parent's house when I was a toddler.

Like many cartoonists these days, I take a couple of weeks off each year and use reruns in the paper. This cartoon originally ran in '89, and I recolored it to use as a vacation rerun in 2001. I still like this gag, and this version looks way better than the original. My favorite touch is the bunny shadow on the floor.

ANSWER TO PAGE 11: Left to right—Tom Wilson, Richard Guindon, Charlie Rodriguez, Mick Stevens, B. Kliban, Gahan Wilson, Ted Rall, Gary Larson, Jack Ziegler, John Callahan, Charles Addams. The one in the water is mine.

ANSWER TO PAGE 14: Twenty-nine—fifteen bunnies, four Easter eggs, one spray bottle of Murphy's Oil Soap, one spider, one ball-peen hammer, a pair of glasses on a bunny, a bow tie on a bunny, a basket in a bunny's hands, an insurance salesman dressed up like a surgeon, a hand under the oxygen tank table, a shoe on top of the cabinets, a live llama in *Sesame Street* boxer shorts locked inside the cabinet behind the anesthesiologist.

ANSWER TO PAGE 19: Waldo is the third-largest rock from the left.

ANSWER TO PAGE 49: Squash, carrots, lima beans.

ANSWER TO PAGE 52: None—Hillbillies are from rural, mountainous areas. Tulsa only had rednecks.

ANSWER TO PAGE 63: I haven't any idea. I don't have anywhere near the time it would take to count up something like that. If you really must have an answer however, use 12,248.

ANSWER TO PAGE 77: It is a strike at a sign making company. If sign painters are on strike, they can't make signs for picketing.

INFO FROM PAGE 111: See page 111 for details.

REASON #1 FROM PAGE 112: Dogs never dress in monochromatic color themes.

REASON #2 FROM PAGE 112: Both are correct, but the spell check on this computer won't recognize the one with a "q."

Recurring Symbols & the Road to Ultimate Bizarro Awareness

If you are a *Bizarro* fan, you "get" things others miss. As you encounter the surreal situations and wackynoids who inhabit your life you think, "this is surreal, they are wacky." You are on the road to ULTIMATE BIZARRO AWARENESS. (UBA)

And so verily, I say unto you, revel in your BIZARRO AWARENESS. You are among the blessed few who see through the yogurt of our earthly existence while most are blind to the everyday weirdness that surrounds them. Forgive them, for they know not how dull they are.

In your daily trudge through the yogurt you may encounter the occasional *Bizarro* joke you do not understand. Chastise yourself not for this state of puzzlement. Walk not through the streets flagellating yourself and crying out to the heavens, "I do not get it, for I am a dullard." Instead, remain quiet, smile and nod knowingly, and just play "find the upside-down bird, pie, eyeball, etc." In truth, even Piraro doesn't get all of the jokes.

The recurring symbols in *Bizarro* cartoons are signposts on the road to UBA. I get many questions from readers regarding the meaning of the recurring symbols in my cartoons. The following explains each signpost and how you can use it to improve the quality of your life and lower your grocery bills.

The Pie of Opportunity

Opportunity is like a piece of pie underfoot. We must watch for it, for if we do not see it, we may step in it and get sticky fruit and crust between our toes. If we search for it wisely, however, open to the possibility that it may be hiding anywhere, we may enjoy the delicious sweetness. But we must not jump hastily at found pie; what at first looks like a scrumptious dessert on the floor may actually be something the cat found under the house.

ACTIVITY TO IMPROVE BIZARRO AWARENESS: Place a fresh piece of pie in the middle of the floor in your home or office. Do not move it and opportunity will knock within twenty-one days. When an opportunity presents itself, eat the pie and share it with the person who brought the opportunity. Do not take "no" for an answer; both of you must finish the pie together or the opportunity will slip away.

The Eyeball of Observation

The eye is a symbol of eternal watchfulness. In each cartoon, the eye is watching the action in the cartoon, and it is watching you read the cartoon. It also watches you watching it watch you and the cartoon. When you watch the eye watching you watch it, you are the watcher and the watched. As you watch the words on this page describing this to you at this very moment, the eye is watching you watch it watch you watching the words.

ACTIVITY: Photocopy and enlarge to life size the drawing of the eyeball on this page (careful, this is copyrighted material and thus this is illegal) and carry it with you always. Place it on tables, counter tops, or floors whenever you interact with people. It will assist you in observing and perceiving your surroundings. Do not explain to anyone why you are doing this.

The Crown of Power

THE CROWN OF POWER AND DUALITY: As in many aspects of our existence, the crown carries dual meaning: good/evil, positive/negative, yin/yang, Fred/Barney. Though the crown is a symbol of power, authority, and wealth. Mayhem can also come from wearing the crown. And "hat hair" is virtually unavoidable.

ACTIVITY: If you are willing to accept these risks and responsibilities, photocopy and enlarge the crown on this page (illegal again) and wear it everywhere you go for ten days to bring you authority, wealth, and power. While you do so you will be invulnerable and your decisions will be absolute and cannot be contradicted. Deal swiftly and harshly with any who criticize.

The Flying Saucer of Possibility

The UFO/ALIEN is a symbol of the immense and immeasurable universe and all its possibilities. As anyone who has ever found themselves at the cold, steely end of an extraterrestrial's medical examination can tell you, aliens are already here and living among us. They are benevolent creatures who wish to study us and learn what they can about our culture. Disguised as earthly creatures of all sorts, they watch us daily. You undoubtedly know many and do not realize it. My Aunt Ruth is an alien. Two of my three brothers-in-law are. Most fast-food workers are, as well as some dogs and all cats. It has been scientifically proven that people who disagree with this are stupid.

ACTIVITY: Photocopy and enlarge the alien on this page and tape him to the inside lining of your jacket. When you suspect someone may be an alien, simply flash the picture where only he/she can see it and say quietly, "You're not fooling me—I know all about you." Use the following chart to judge whether or not they are extraterrestrial by their response.
Denial: yes
Confusion: yes
Hostility: yes
Ignore you: probably
Laugh in your face: definitely
Full confession: definitely not

The Mysteries of K²

K is the eleventh letter in the English alphabet.
An eleven is drawn with two ones.
Eleven plus two is thirteen, a traditionally unlucky number.
Eleven minus two, twice, is seven, a traditionally lucky number.

Other interesting connections between K and 2:
- K9 is slang for canine, the world's most popular and cherished pet.
- I have two daughters whose names both begin with K (Kloorfit and Krullbeck).
- The names Kruschev and Kennedy both start with K.
- The second entry in the dictionary under K is "Kaaba," the sacred Muslim shrine in Mecca. "Kaaba" has two a's in a row; "Mecca" has two c's in a row. C is the third letter in the alphabet.
- Eleven plus three is fourteen, the exact number of days in two weeks.

Coincidence?

ACTIVITY: Carry a notepad with you and write down all the connections between the letter K and the number two that occur to you each day. Discuss your list at length with everyone you know.

The Lost Loafer

In life, all of us understand what it is to be lost: literally lost, in the lingerie department of a store, or figuratively lost, not knowing which way to turn in life, which job to take, which country's customs officials are easiest to sneak live animals past. The loafer is in recognition of that feeling we all have at some time in all our lives: useless, outcast, purposeless.

ACTIVITY: The next time you are driving and you see a single shoe in the street, pick it up and carry it with you proudly while keeping an eye out for its mate. Feed it, bathe it, give it a name. Introduce it to people you meet as if it were a cherished old friend. It is no less than you would like someone to do for you.

The Bunny of Exuberance

In all of us resides a little child with an overwhelming sense of wonder and exuberance for life. As we grow older, our hearts, minds, and souls harden and become brittle. Some even mildew. To achieve UBA, we must remain in touch with the child within us to keep a fresh outlook on life. The bunny, peeking his cute little furry head up from some unexpected place is that child within you. The child that you used to be—frightened, loving, innocent, immature, hyperactive, unable to control your bladder. To achieve UBA, we must stay in touch with the Bunny inside us.

ACTIVITY TO IMPROVE BIZARRO AWARENESS: Photocopy and enlarge dozens of copies of the Bunny and hide him in unlikely places throughout each day. Whenever someone comes across the bunny and asks about it, encourage them to abandon self-conciousness and act childishly along with you. A good place to begin is by playing naked in a public fountain.

The Arrow of Vulnerability

In some *Bizarro* cartoons there appears a character with an arrow in his or her back. This arrow is to remind us all of our vulnerability. No matter how strong we are we all have a blind spot that can be attacked and conquered by those who are out of our view. This is one of the many things that connect us with each other as humans: We all need each other to watch our backsides. I watch many backsides daily and always feel enriched for it.

ACTIVITY: With an indelible marker, draw a large arrow on the back of all your shirts to remind you of your vulnerability. Poke your friends and coworkers in the back with a sharpened pencil to remind them of theirs.

The Inverted Bird

The bird is the primary symbol of UBA. Birds are creatures of great visual beauty (except for chickens) and of enchanting musical ability (except for chickens). They are creatures that can both walk in the dirt with the lowliest of worms and soar through the heavens, high above the muck and din of modern life. The *Bizarro* bird is represented upside-down to show the importance of individuality. The person on the road to UBA does not march with the rest of the band: neatly in line, wearing identical uniforms, playing the same notes at the same time. Rather, the BIZARRO AWARE marches to his/her own drum, wears his/her own costume, moves against the tide of other players, undaunted by the occasional trombone slide to the jaw or bass drum mallet to the midsection. The person on the road to UBA proudly hangs upside-down, wearing a funny hat.

ACTIVITY:
Tie a funny hat to your head and hang upside-down out of the window of your home or office. Shout "I can fly high above the muck and din of modern life. I am on the road to BIZARRO AWARENESS." Using the simple instructions below, learn to draw the *Bizarro* bird and use it in place of your signature for the rest of your life.

Step 1. Draw a 'Y.' 1. Y

Step 3. Repeat steps 1 and 2. 3. YY

Step 2. Draw a line in the middle of the 'Y.' 2. Y

Step 4. Draw a bird below that, with a little hat. 4. YY

The Fish of Humility

Fish is brain food. It nourishes the body and mind and is exceptionally low in saturated fat. But fish can also be humbling. Catching one can be an arduous and frustrating task involving patience, huge rubber boots, thousands of dollars of equipment, and a lot of beer. Fish can be amazingly difficult to outwit, and yet they have a brain the size of a Rice Krispy.

ACTIVITY: Photocopy and enlarge the fish on this page and carry it with you always. Use it to order fish in restaurants where the wait staff do not speak your language.

About the Author

Standing 600' 7" above sea level at his home in Dallas, Dan Piraro makes people at sea level seem small and insignificant. He is not a tall man, and rarely makes anyone seem small or insignificant in person, so little ideas like this are sadly important to him.

He has two daughters, two dogs, two kidneys, two wheels on his nifty Vespa, two consecutive Reuben awards (cartooning's highest accolade), and only one desire: for every person in the world to give him just one dollar. If you met him you would probably feel sorry for him and give him even more.

Drawing *Bizarro* is a fun job and he is really very thankful to God and everyone for being able to do it. He would like to thank you for buying his bologna.

Dan Piraro can be hired to speak to groups and organizations of any kind and he is funny as hell. See Bizarro.com for details.